NORTH AMERICA'S
BIGGEST BEASTS

CARIBOU

Joyce Jeffries

PowerKiDS press.

New York

Published in 2016 by The Rosen Publishing Group, Inc.
29 East 21st Street, New York, NY 10010

First Edition

Editor: Katie Kawa
Book Design: Reann Nye

Photo Credits: Cover (background), p. 14 John E Marriott/All Canada Photos/Getty Images; cover (caribou), p. 1 Iakov Filimonov/Shutterstock.com; pp. 4, 17 Dmitry Chulov/Shutterstock.com; pp. 5, 12, 21 Sergey Krasnoshchokov/Shutterstock.com; p. 6 Joyce Marrero/Shutterstock.com; p. 7 Josef Pittner/Shutterstock.com; pp. 8–9 Andrey Gontarev/Shutterstock.com; p. 9 (map) boreala/Shutterstock.com; p. 10 Mark Hamblin/age fotostock/Getty Images; p. 11 Sethislav/Shutterstock.com; p. 13 Cultura RM/Art Wolfe Stock/Cultura/Getty Images; p.15 Roberta Olenick/All Canada Photos/Getty Images; p. 16 saraporn/Shutterstock.com; p. 18 (golden eagle) yykkaa/Shutterstock.com; p. 18 (wolf) Holly Kuchera/Shutterstock.com; p. 19 NancyS/Shutterstock.com; p. 20 Tyler McKay/Shutterstock.com; p. 22 Sylvie Bouchard/Shutterstock.com.

Cataloging-in-Publication Data

Jeffries, Joyce.
Caribou / by Joyce Jeffries.
p. cm. — (North America's biggest beasts)
Includes index.
ISBN 978-1-5081-4285-0 (pbk.)
ISBN 978-1-5081-4286-7 (6-pack)
ISBN 978-1-5081-4291-1 (library binding)
1. Caribou — Juvenile literature. I. Jeffries, Joyce. II. Title.
QL737.U55 J44 2016
599.65'8—d23

Manufactured in the United States of America

CPSIA Compliance Information: Batch #BW16PK: For Further Information contact Rosen Publishing, New York, New York at 1-800-237-9932

CONTENTS

Wild Reindeer

In the coldest parts of North America, huge deer travel thousands of miles each year to find food and have babies. These deer are caribou, and they're known for having one of the longest **migrations** of large **mammals** on Earth. In fact, one kind of caribou can travel over 3,000 miles (4,828 km) each year.

Another kind of caribou goes by a name people know very well—reindeer! Reindeer are smaller caribou raised by humans in Europe, Asia, and some parts of North America.

THE BIG IDEA

Caribou are sometimes called "wild reindeer."

Caribou are huge mammals that travel in huge groups, which are called herds. Some herds are believed to be made up of over 500,000 caribou.

Amazing Antlers

Caribou are much larger than the deer many people see in their backyard. They can weigh as much as 700 pounds (317.5 kg)! Female caribou are smaller than males. Also, caribou that live farther south are often larger than those that live in more northern areas.

Caribou are known for their large **antlers**. Unlike other kinds of deer, both male and female caribou grow antlers. The antlers of adult male caribou are much longer than those of female caribou.

THE BIG IDEA

Adult caribou generally stand between 4 and 5 feet (1.2 and 1.5 m) tall at the shoulder.

The antlers of an adult male caribou can grow to be over 4 feet (1.2 m) long.

male caribou

female caribou

A Circumpolar Creature

Caribou live in northern areas of many countries in North America, Europe, and Asia. In North America, they're mainly found in Alaska and Canada. A very small group of caribou also live in northern parts of Idaho and Montana.

Caribou once had a much larger **range**. They used to live as far south as Maine in the United States, as well as in areas of Germany, Great Britain, and Poland in Europe. However, people in those areas took over their **habitats**. Overhunting also led to the disappearance of caribou from these places.

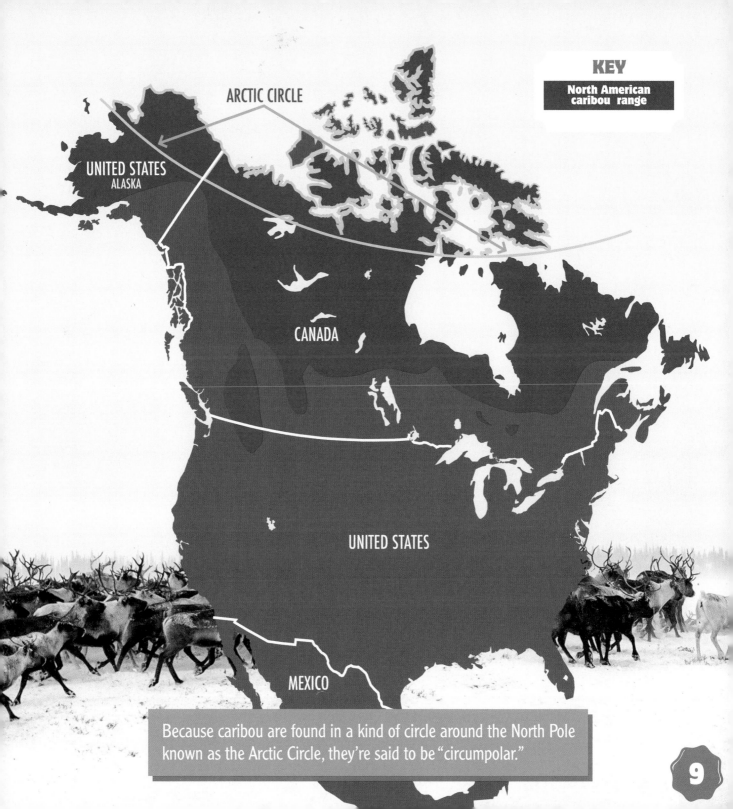

KEY

North American
caribou range

ARCTIC CIRCLE

UNITED STATES
ALASKA

CANADA

UNITED STATES

MEXICO

Because caribou are found in a kind of circle around the North Pole known as the Arctic Circle, they're said to be "circumpolar."

Helpful Hoofs

A caribou's large body has **adapted** to life on the move through harsh landscapes that are often covered with snow and ice. The fur on a caribou traps heat close to its body. Caribou fur is often darker in color the farther south the animal lives.

Perhaps the caribou's greatest adaptation for life in its cold habitat is its hoofs. Each of a caribou's feet has two hoofs. Caribou have the largest hoofs of any kind of deer. Their large size supports the caribou as it stands in the snow.

A caribou's hoofs are 3 to 4 inches (7.6 to 10.2 cm) long and 4 to 5 inches (10.2 to 12.7 cm) wide. Their large size and special shape help caribou move around in the snow and ice.

large size helps support the weight of a caribou's body in snow, much like snowshoes support a person's weight

wide shape helps caribou swim

HOW DO HOOFS HELP CARIBOU?

sharp edges help caribou grip rocks and ice

bottom is hollow and curved in, which is useful for digging in the snow for food

Massive Mammal Migration

In the summer months, caribou live in the northernmost part of their range. This is where baby caribou, which are called calves, are born. However, these northern areas have very harsh weather in the winter. This is why caribou **migrate** to warmer areas in the fall. The first big snowfall of the year is often their sign to begin their migration.

When the weather begins to get warmer in the spring, caribou start to migrate again. This time, they return north to their summer range.

THE BIG IDEA

Caribou can run at speeds of up to 50 miles (80 km) per hour during their migrations.

The summer ranges of caribou are often called calving grounds. This name comes from the fact that calves are born and raised in these areas.

13

Caribou Calves

Caribou **mate** in the fall. This mating season is known as the rut. During the rut, male caribou fight with each other. This fighting sometimes leads to male caribou getting hurt.

Baby caribou are born on calving grounds in the spring. Most female caribou only have one calf at a time. Calves can stand on their own minutes after they're born. Just one day after their birth, they can run faster than a person! Like other mammals, calves drink milk from their mother as they grow.

A caribou calf can weigh as much as 26 pounds (12 kg) at birth. That's a big baby!

Huge Herbivores

While calves drink milk from their mother at first, they soon begin to eat grasses. Caribou are herbivores, which are animals that eat only plants. Because caribou are such large animals, they can eat up to 12 pounds (5.4 kg) of food each day.

The kinds of plants caribou eat depend on the season. In the summer, they eat leaves, grasses, and many other plants they find on the ground. In the winter, they eat whatever plants and **lichens** they can find in the snow.

Caribou eat more during the summer months because food is easier to find. This helps fatten them up for winter, when they have to dig through the snow to find food.

Caribou in Danger

Caribou only eat plants, but many animals like to eat caribou! Grizzly bears hunt caribou in warmer months. Wolf packs hunt these animals in the winter. People also hunt caribou for their meat and for sport. They've been hunting these animals for thousands of years.

Calves are in the most danger of being killed by other animals. In fact, many calves die within their first year. Golden eagles hunt calves in the summer, and lynx hunt them in the fall.

golden eagle

wolf

THE BIG IDEA

Traveling in large herds helps caribou stay safe. Many caribou can look out for predators as they migrate together.

Although many calves are killed by predators during their first year, caribou can live up to 15 years in the wild.

Caribou and People

   In North America, there are around 3.5 million caribou living in the wild. That may seem like a large number, but caribou are actually **endangered** in all areas of the United States except for Alaska. Overhunting has played a part in the shrinking number of caribou in North America. Building projects and oil drilling in caribou habitats have also harmed these animals.

   However, there's still a large number of caribou living in Alaska. Almost 1 million caribou call Alaska home.

oil drilling

THE BIG IDEA

People in Alaska hunt and kill around 22,000 caribou each year.

Over 30 different herds of caribou live in Alaska. This is the one place in the United States where caribou aren't endangered.

Bigger Is Better

Caribou know that bigger is often better in the animal world. They have big bodies that have adapted to their harsh habitat. Their large hoofs help them swim and walk through the snow. They also travel in big numbers to stay safe from predators.

Whether it's the large herds in Alaska, the endangered groups, or even reindeer—all caribou are amazing animals. They stick together to travel far and have big bodies built for their long journeys.

Glossary

adapt: To change to fit new conditions.

antler: One of the bony horns on a deer.

endangered: Threatened with dying out.

habitat: The natural home for plants, animals, and other living things.

lichen: A plantlike living thing that grows on rocks and the bark of trees.

mammal: Any warm-blooded animal whose babies drink milk and whose body is covered with hair or fur.

mate: To come together to make babies.

migrate: To move from one place to another as the seasons change.

migration: The movement of animals from one place to another as the seasons change.

range: An open area of land over which animals move and feed.

Index

A
adults, 6, 7
Alaska, 8, 20, 21, 22
antlers, 6, 7
Arctic Circle, 9

B
building projects, 20

C
calves, 12, 13, 14, 15, 16, 18, 19
calving grounds, 13, 14
Canada, 8

D
deer, 4, 6, 10

F
females, 6, 7, 14
food, 4, 11, 16, 17
fur, 10

H
habitats, 8, 10, 20, 22
herbivores, 16
herds, 5, 18, 21, 22
hoofs, 10, 11, 22

I
ice, 10, 11

M
males, 6, 7, 14
mammal, 4, 5, 14
mating season, 14
migration, 4, 12, 18

O
oil drilling, 20
overhunting, 8, 20

P
predators, 18, 19, 22

R
range, 8, 12, 13
reindeer, 4, 22
rut, 14

S
snow, 10, 11, 12, 16, 17, 22

U
United States, 8, 20, 21

Websites

Due to the changing nature of Internet links, PowerKids Press has developed an online list of websites related to the subject of this book. This site is updated regularly. Please use this link to access the list: www.powerkidslinks.com/nabb/carib